BRITISH RAILWAY POSTCARDS OF YESTERYEAR

LONDON

IAN ALLAN LTD

Introduction

In the early years of the century and, indeed, even before that, postcard collecting was almost as great a hobby as philately and the card producers were quick to see the possibilities in the railway field. Large numbers of cards seem to have reached the market but by our standards most of the illustrations were somewhat poor until the advent of 'F Moore' and the Locomotive Publishing Company.

As far as can be traced, there was no such person as a Mr F Moore and it is believed that the many illustrations bearing his monicker were, in fact, created by several people, one certainly was Mr M Secretan, though very little trace of him or his colleagues can be found. Many of the originals are oil paintings over a photograph base, hence the accuracy of the illustrations.

This book, which is in some way complementary to the companion volume covering pre-Grouping timetable maps, comprises a random selection of F Moore pictures and has been organised into sections relating to appropriate pre-Grouping companies, whilst in the last pages we have included some Irish and Continental pictures as well as a few non-F Moore's to demonstrate the interest in railways at the time of publication — "Railways in the Thirties", of course, relates to the 1830s.

When the Locomotive Publishing Co was taken over by Ian Allan Ltd in the 1950s a set of very ancient 3-colour printing blocks was found and much to everyone's delight, it was discovered that these were quite printable and by the skill of a local printer — Clare O'Molesey — about fifty cards were re-printed. Alas, thereafter the blocks were mislaid, though it is doubtful whether there are now any letterpress printers left who could reproduce them. However, modern technology has enabled us to reproduce from the *original* cards and we are able thereby to provide what we hope will be an interesting and even exciting look backwards at the super works of those who worked so brilliantly with the name of F Moore for the Locomotive Publishing Company all those years ago.

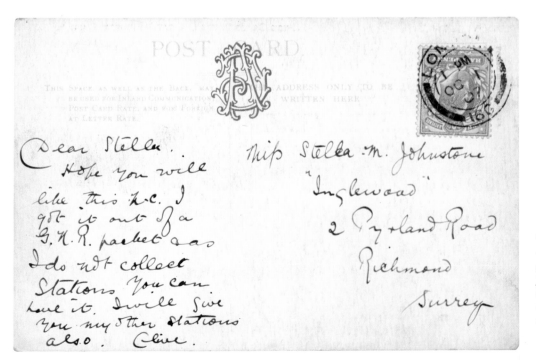

The postcard collecting hobby was not restricted to the male genus. Miss Stella M Johnstone seems to have been an avid collector of railway cards. Note the postage was only $\frac{1}{2}$ d in 1907.

RAILWAYS IN THE 'THIRTIES'.

SANKEY VALLEY VIADUCT.

Engineering structures were featured in the LNWR's series "Railways in the Thirties" and here we see the new form of transport racing above the old on the Sankey Valley Viaduct. This is not an F Moore.

POST CARD

(FOR ADDRESS ONLY.)

"The London & North Western Railway is noted for Punctuality, Speed, Smooth Riding, Dustless Tracks, Safety and Comfort, and is the Oldest Established Firm in the Railway Passenger Business."

Buy the L. & N. W. Series of Pictorial Postcards. 2d. per set of six different cards. Over 5½ millions sold.

McCorquodale & Co., Limited.

Here is the reverse side of the Sankey Viaduct card. The postcards were 2d for a set of six and over 5$\frac{1}{2}$ million copies had been sold. Interestingly McCorquodale & Co printed the first Ian Allan books too!

All the captions printed in this book are the original wordage printed either on the face or reverse of the original cards, though perhaps some older readers may not concur with the sentiments expressed in the last picture. Obviously prepared by the LNWR Company.

G.W.R.—Bristol Station.

GWR Bristol Station

GWR *"Iron Duke"* class 4-2-2
with broad gauge express
near Uffington c1890

GW Dean 4-2-2 with up
Worcester express near Hayes
c1910

PLYMOUTH EXPRESS. G.W.R.

The ''Cornish Riviera Express''

GWR up Birkenhead Breakfast Car Express near Ruislip, locomotive *County of Merioneth*

GWR down ''Cornishman'' near Acton c1900

4.4.0 Express Engine, "Stanley Baldwin," starting from Paddington.

GWR 4-4-0 Express engine
Stanley Baldwin starting from
Paddington

Shrub Hill Station, Worcester.

GWR Shrub Hill Station
Worcester

GWR 4-6-0 on up West of
England Express passing
Acton

GWR "Saint" class 4-6-0 with down express approaching Twyford c1912

GWR up Birmingham Express near Ruislip

The Great Bear with the "Plymouth Limited" leaving London

GWR Hospital Train

GWR 4-6-0 No 2902 on an up
Birmingham express near
Ruislip

GWR interior of Old Oak
Locomotive Depot London

Gret Western Express (at Dawlish)

GWR 4-cylinder De Glehn compound express locomotive. Built at Belfort (France) 1905. Named *Alliance* in 1908 — scrapped 1929

GWR No 111 *Great Bear*. The first ''Pacific' type locomotive to run in Great Britain. Built at Swindon 1908. converted to standard 4-6-0 and renamed *Viscount Churchill* in 1924

GWR 4-4-0 express passenger
Locomotive No 4107
Cineraria built in Swindon
1908 — scrapped 1927

GWR 4-6-0 4-cylinder No 4073
Caerphilly Castle

SIX COUPLED BOGIE EXPRESS LOCOMOTIVE, GREAT WESTERN RAILWAY.

GWR 4-6-0 No 175 *Viscount
Churchill* designed by G J
Churchward, built at Swindon
1905

LSWR up Plymouth Express
passing Surbiton

LSWR Class D15 4-4-0 No 466
with a down West of England
Express in Clapham Cutting
c1914

LSWR North Devon Express

Exeter Station.—London and South Western Railway.

Exeter Station-London &
South Western Railway

LSWR 4-6-0 No 443 on down
Bournemouth express

LSWR up Bude Express

LSWR 4-6-0 no 443

The Bournemouth Express —
distance from London to
Bournemouth 108 miles is
covered by the London &
South Western Railway
Express in 2 hours and 6
minutes

LSWR Class H15 4-6-0 No 486
designed by R W Urie, built at
Eastleigh in 1914

LBSCR Class H2 4-4-2 No 422 with "Southern Belle" leaving Victoria c1914

LBSCR "Southern Belle" at Victoria Station

LBSCR Class H1 4-4-2 No 40 with down "Southern Belle" passing Balham Intermediate signalbox c1910

LBSCR Victoria Station London in 1908

L.B. & S.C.R. and L. & N.W.R.   Liverpool to Brighton Express passing Wandsworth.

LBSCR and LNWR Liverpool to Brighton Express passing Wandsworth

LBSCR "Southern Belle" London-Brighton 60 minute express

MR. STROUDLEY'S SIX COUPLED TANK, L.B. & S.C.R.

Terrier Class

DENMARK 39

Built at Brighton by W Stroudley 1878   List 191   50 engines built
DW 4ft   Cyl 13×20   HS 518   SP   1872 to 1880
Weight 24-7-0-0   Coal 27 Cft   Water 500 gals

LBSCR Mr Stroudley's six-coupled tank ("Terrier" class)

MR. STROUDLEY'S SINGLE EXPRESS, L.B. & S.C.R.

LBSCR Mr Stroudley's single express locomotive

LBSCR Class B1 0-4-2 No 175 *Hayling* designed by W Stroudley, built at Brighton 1890

LBSCR Mr Billinton's four-coupled express

LBSCR Class E5 0-6-2T No 584 *Lordington* designed by R J Billinton, built at Brighton 1903

LBSCR Class H1 4-4-2 No 40 with express train c1910

LBSCR No 4-6-2 Tank No 325 *Abergavenny*

LBSCR No 327 *Charles C Macrae* 4-6-4 Express Tank Locomotive

LBSCR up Express headed by Class B4 4-4-0 No 54 *Empress* leaving Clayton Tunnel

SECR Dover boat express

SECR Boat express nearing Sandling Junction

SECR Hastings station departure platform

SECR Class D 4-4-0 No 145 with Hastings "Car Train" c1905

SECR Charing Cross Station 1907

SECR Wainwright Class E 4-4-0 No 516 Folkestone express passing Elmstead Woods c1910

Royal Engine, S.E. & C.Ry., No. 516. Franco-British Exhibition, 1908.

SECR Royal Engine No 516
Franco-British Exhibition
1908

Metropolitan Railway electric
locomotive No 17 with a
Rickmansworth train c1925

Metropolitan Railway 0-6-4
Tank No 94 *Lord Aberconway*

LTS 4-4-2T No 90 *Thundersley* with a Southend-Fenchurch St train c1910

LTS Southend Express. A favourite express from Fenchurch Street Station London to Southend completing the journey in about 40 minutes

LTS 4-4-2T No 80 *Southend on Sea* designed by T Whitelegg, built by R Stephenson and exhibited at the International Exhibition, Shepherds Bush 1909. later renamed *Thundersley*

GER Continental Express near Brentwood

GER Southend train near Brentwood

GER "Claud Hamilton" class 4-4-0 with an up express descends Brentwood bank c1910

GER Lowestoft & Yarmouth
Restaurant Car Express

GER Rebuilt Class T19 4-4-0
and passenger train crossing
Trowse swing bridge

Fenchurch Street Station

GE 2-4-0 locomotive No 761
(decorated for a royal
occasion)

GER 4-4-0 Express engine
No 1831

GER 4-6-0 No 1500

Spilsby Station, Lincs, GNR in 1870. One of the original 50 locomotives built by Sharp Bros in 1847 and converted to tank engines for branch line traffic

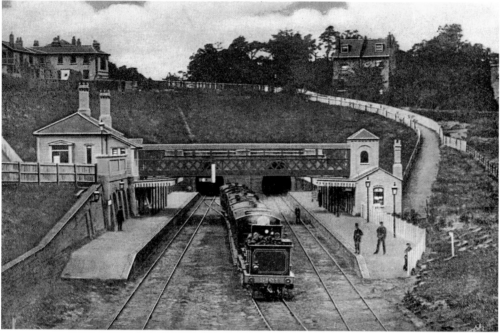

GN suburban train at Highgate in the 1880s

GNR local train leaving King's Cross

The "Flying Scotsman" passing Hadley Wood

GNR King's Cross Station by night — 4-4-0 No 1378 Class D1

GNR A down Scottish express climbing the Northern Heights on the outskirts of London, double-headed by a 2-2-2 and a 4-2-2

GNR 4-2-2 No 215 designed by A Sturrock built by R and W Hawthorn 1853

GNR 4-2-2 No 1007 designed by P Stirling, built at Doncaster 1895

GNR 4-6-2 three-cylinder express No 1470. Diameter of coupled wheels 68". Cylinders 20" x 26". Heating surface 2,533sq ft

GNR Leeds Dining Car
express passing Hadley Wood
tunnel

GNR Atlantic type express
locomotive with Walschaert
valve gear. Built at Doncaster
1907. Converted to standard
2-cylinder compound 1920.
now LNER 4421

GNR 0-8-0 No 455 designed
by H A Ivatt, built at
Doncaster 1909

GCR Sheffield Express

LNER (Great Central Section) local train

GCR High Wycombe train leaving Marylebone

GCR Ambulance train —
Robinson "Director" 4-4-0
No 431 Class 11E *Edwin A
Beazley*. Built Gorton 1913

GCR 4-4-2 with a down
express composed of
clerestory stock in brown and
cream livery c1908

Sheffield & Manchester
Express at Marylebone Station

LNER ex-GC 4-cylinder *Lord Faringdon* class 4-6-0 with express train shortly after the Grouping 1923

GCR Manchester-Sheffield expresses passing at entrance to woodhead tunnel

GCR Sheffield & Manchester Express near Gerrards Cross

GCR 4-6-0 Express passenger
locomotive No 423 *Sir Sam
Fay*, built at Gorton 1912
(now LNER 5423)

GCR 4-6-2 No 165 designed
by J G Robinson, built at
Gorton 1911

Great Central Express Engine

L&NER (North eastern section) Newcastle to Liverpool 'Express passing over Wiske Moor Troughs

North Eastern Express

NER Leeds-Scarborough 'Express at 80 miles per hour

NER ''Newcastle'' express
leaving Edinburgh

York Station-East Coast
Express leaving

NER Leeds to Edinburgh
Express

NER 825 4-6-0 Express Goods Locomotive with Stumpf cylinders. Built Darlington 1913. Converted to standard type 1924. Now LNER 825

NER 4-4-0 Express passenger locomotive No 1238 built at Darlington 1908. (Now LNER 1238)

NER 4-cylinder 4-4-2 passenger express locomotive No 730 built at Gateshead 1906 — scrapped 1934

LNER (H&B Section) 4-4-0 Express

H&BR 0-8-0 No 117. Built by Yorkshire Engine Co, Sheffield in 1907

Midland 4-4-0 No 14 designed by S W Johnson, rebuilt by R M Deeley

Midland Railway Station, Gloucester.

Leaving St. Pancras — Midland Railway.

Midland Railway Station, Gloucester

MR — leaving St Pancras

MR — 11.50am Scotch Corridor Express

LEEDS AND BRADFORD EXPRESS, M.R.

MR — Leeds and Bradford
Express

MR — Leeds and Bradford
Express

MR 3-cylinder 4-4-0 No 1013
heads a down express near
Mill Hill c1910

MR 3-cylinder compound express No 1000

MR "4" 4-4-0 No 999 designed by R M Deeley built at Derby 1907

MR (LTSR Section) 4-6-4 Tank No 2101

Somerset and Dorset Joint Railway – No. 77 Express Engine.

Somerset & Dorset Joint
Railway No 77 Express Engine

On the Manifold Valley Light Railway, Derbyshire, near Beeston Tor.   (North Staffordshire Railway).

On the Manifold Valley Light
Railway, Derbyshire near
Beeston Tor (North
Staffordshire Railway)

NSR 4-4-0 Express passenger
locomotive No 86, built at
Stoke 1910, scrapped 1929

Express Locomotive, Midland and Great Northern Joint Railway.

Express Locomotive, Midland & Great Northern Joint Railway

M&GNJR 4-4-2 Tank Locomotive No 9, built at Melton Constable in 1909

M&GN 4-4-0 No 53
S W Jackson design, rebuilt with large boiler and Belpaire firebox 1910

L&YR Leeds-Blackpool
express

L&Y 4-cylinder 4-6-0 with
Newcastle-Liverpool express
composed of NE stock on
Walkden troughs c1910

LNWR No 3020 *Cornwall*

LNWR "Wild Irishman" —
The 8.30am Irish-daylight mail
from Euston, familiarly
termed "Wild Irishman" and
its counterpart starting at
8.45pm cover the 264 miles to
Holyhead in about five and
one half hours. The long
stages between Rugby, Crewe
and 'Chester, the only stops,
are made possible by means
of frequent water-troughs
from which engines pick up
water without slackening
speed

LNWR Express passing over
water troughs at Bushey

LNW Experiment class 4-6-0
with west coast express at
Shap, and aeroplane

LNW 4-cylinder Claughton
class 4-6-0 with an up express
leaving Carlisle Citadel Station
in 1914

L. & N. W. Railway. Local Train near Harrow.

LNWR local train near Harrow

LNWR — Standedge Tunnel

LNW ''Precursor'' class 4-4-0 with an up express on Bushey troughs c1910

Scotch express leaving Euston in 1905

LMSR (NW section) down Birmingham express

LNWR up express passing
Bushey troughs

LNWR 4-6-0 express passenger
locomotive No 1987
Glendower built at Crewe
1906. (Now LMSR 25466)

CR — 2pm Express from
Glasgow Central, near
Eglinton Street

"HIGHLAND EXPRESS
CALEDONIAN RLY

CR — Highland Express

Caledonian 4-6-0 No 903
Cardean with an up west
coast express near Beattock
c1910

Corridor Express, Caledonian Railway, leaving Stirling.

CR corridor express leaving
Stirling

CR 4-6-0 express passenger locomotive No 50 *Sir James Thompson*, built at Glasgow 1902. (Now LMSR 14751)

CR 4-6-0 built at St Rollox 1913. (Now LMSR 17905)

Waverley Station, Edinburgh

NBR 4-4-2 No 868
Aberdonian with set train
built for the Edinburgh-
Aberdeen service 1906

N.B. Railway.—Express leaving Edinburgh.

NBR — Express leaving
Edinburgh

North British Express

North British Express

LNER (North British Section)
West Highland express
Glenfinnan Station

NBR Waverley Express

N.E.R. East Coast Express leaving Waverley Station, Edinburgh.

NER east coast express leaving
Waverley Station, Edinburgh

GSWR 4-6-4T No 545
designed by R H Whitelegg,
built by the North British
Locomotive Co Ltd 1922

GSWR 4-6-0 Express No 386

GSWR Glasgow Express. One
of the many express trains run
over the Glasgow and South
Western and Midland routes
between Glasgow and
London. The carriages are all
of the corridor type and
dining cars for both first and
third class passengers are
provided. Locomotive No 11
is a four-cylinder engine built
by the G & SW Rly Co

Great North of Scotland Railway passenger locomotive No 41, built 1864 to designs of Mr Cowan, locomotive supt. Modification made by Mr Pickersgill. The oldest locomotive still in service on the L&NER

HR 4-6-0 No 145 *Murthly Castle*, built Glasgow 1900, scrapped 1930

Great North of Scotland Railway — Royal Train

Midland (NCC) 4-4-0 and passenger train, Belfast-Portrush service c1907

Cork & Macroom Direct railway 0-6-2 Tank, built by Andrew Barclay Sons & Co Ltd, Kilmarnock, Scotland

Bombay-Poona Mail. The magnificent train which carries His Majesty's mails between these two towns on the Great Indian Peninsula Railway is one of the finest trains in the British Empire. It was used by T. R. H. The Prince and Princess of Wales during their recent tour of India

The Khedive's Special. This engine and carriage were built by R Stephenson & Sons in 1862, and are used by the Khedive of Egypt when he moves his Court between his summer palace of Montaza and Alexandria.

LB&SCR. A relic of the past.

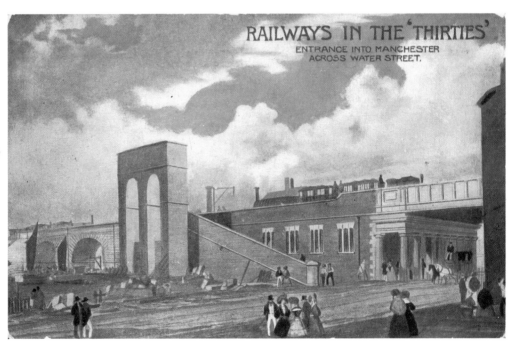

"The London & North Western Railway is noted for Punctuality, Speed, Smooth Riding, Dustless Tracks, Safety and Comfort and is the Oldest Established Firm in the Railway Passenger Business".

An advert for F. Moore's railway photographs which appeared in 1935.

First published 1991

ISBN 0 7110 2018 3

Published by Ian Allan Ltd, Shepperton, Surrey; and phototypeset and printed by Ian Allan Printing Ltd at their works at Coombelands in Runnymede, England